Sat 25/11.00
Bushey
Book Fair.
Codex/00

Railway
Outred
Commercial
Vehicles.

RAILWAY-OWNED
COMMERCIAL
VEHICLES

S.W.STEVENS-STRATTEN & W.J.ALDRIDGE

LONDON

IAN ALLAN LTD

© Ian Allan Ltd 1987

Published by Ian Allan Ltd, Shepperton, Surrey; and printed by Ian Allan Printing Ltd at their works at Coombelands in Runnymede, England

Above:
A conventional advertising van is illustrated by this Ford Model Y delivered in November 1934, here photographed at Marylebone but used in Manchester until 1947. The LNER also used Austin 10cwt vans for publicity work.
Ian Allan Library

Front cover, top left:
Battery-electric vehicle, now preserved by the National Railway Museum. *G. Arnold*

Front cover, top right:
The ubiquitous Scammell mechanical horse and van trailer.

Front cover, bottom:
Thornycroft Sturdy dropside lorry supplied to the LNER in 1937. *Ian Allan Library*

Contents

Back cover, top:
Thornycroft 10-ton dropside lorry in the service of the GWR. *LPC/Ian Allan Library*

Back cover, centre left:
Austin flat-bed lorry in temporary trouble at a country station. *W. J. Aldridge*

Back cover, centre right:
Two Austin vans. *W. J. Aldridge*

Back cover, bottom:
Scammell 6-ton mechanical horse in wartime livery with lady driver. *Ian Allan Library*

the total carrying capacity of his vehicles; while a B licence restricted a haulier's operation to local work and a C licence allowed only a manufacturer's own goods to be carried on its vehicles. The railways were entitled to object to the granting of additional A licences and thereby restrict road competition.

Despite this stricture on road hauliers, the railways still laboured under a duty to carry whatever goods were offered to them — a concept known as the Common Carrier Obligation. In granting this monopolistic condition, Parliament had insisted that the railways publish their standard rate tariff. To some extent this enabled road hauliers to undercut the equivalent railway charges, although there were thousands of exceptional railway rates which were not published so the hauliers would offer a different or higher level of service, and possibly at an increased price. The restrictions covering the railway rates did not apply to road hauliers, nor did the Common Carrier liability; thus they were able to cream off some of the profitable traffic.

The railway management were certainly full of new ideas and used their new found powers to offer additional services to manufacturers, such as Country Lorry Services, Railhead Distribution, Warehousing and Contract Hire. There were also plans to eliminate double handling of traffic, by closing some of the smaller cartage depots and using road motors for linking journeys between larger goods depots.

It is very important to note that the road cartage operation in itself was not expected to make a profit. Cartage was regarded as an ancillary service designed to attract traffic to the railway by offering door-to-door transit, and the profit would be made on the rail portion of the transit. The railways, however, were still convinced that their overall poor financial position was due to unfettered road competition and the obligation of being a common carrier. To emphasise this they opened the 'Square Deal' campaign in the mid-1930s, which sought freedom from pricing and product constraints. In a nutshell, they wanted to obtain an economic price from each service or abandon it, which would have involved closing down many facilities. With the outbreak of the war the whole competitive aspect of road versus rail was forgotten and, in fact, the abilities of the Ministry of War Transport staff, in combining the facilities of road and rail, were treated as a prototype for the nationalisation plans of the Labour Party. The constraints on pricing were finally removed by the Transport Act of 1953, but the gain was very shortlived, because that same Act de nationalised a large part of British Road Services, which then became a competitor to the railways rather than the partner envisaged under the 1948 Nationalisation Act.

This Act of 1948 had brought together a very mixed cartage fleet of some 13,000 road motor vehicles, plus some horses, with grandiose plans for co-ordination between the railways and road hauliers. As noted above, this was not to be, and by 1954, with a fleet of 15,000 vehicles, the railways were once again fighting the road hauliers.

The Railway Modernisation Plan of 1955 gave an optimistic view of the continuance of the railway's cartage operation. A total of £50 million was allocated for the reconstruction and mechanisation of freight terminals and the closure of old depots. Another £10 million was allowed for new handling equipment and road vehicles.

Despite this investment the cartage operations remained unprofitable, with the 'smalls' traffic being the main culprit. Among the reasons for non-profitability were under-pricing, over-manning, poor productivity of men and equipment and excessive delivery delays. By 1962 the overall situation had worsened considerably and the 'Sundries Plan' of that year envisaged the cartage operations reduced from over 1,000 depots to just 244 large depots. The 1962 Transport Act re-introduced a restriction on railway vehicles carrying goods throughout by road without the express permission of the Minister of Transport, but this requirement was later withdrawn under the 1967 Transport Act.

The report entitled 'Reshaping of the Railways' — generally known as the Beeching Plan — was published in 1963 and agreed to the cut backs in the Sundries Plan of 1962, but failed to improve the productivity of the freight operations. Further retrenchment was necessary and plans were made to enable British Railways to withdraw from the cartage market. Two specific decisions were made by Beeching. First, in future all goods traffic would only be carried in full train-loads and, second, anthing less than train-load traffic would only be carried in large containers, on Liner Trains running to fixed timetables between a few main depots. As a result, cartage traffic was rapidly abandoned, generally by the simple expedient of closing goods depots. Following the 1968 Transport Act,

Above left:
One of the early steam lorries operated before World War 1 by the London & North Western Railway. Note the steel tyres.
Real Photographs

Right:
The Great Western was among the first companies to operate petrol-engined vehicles; and this is believed to be No 6 in its fleet in 1904.
BR/Ian Allan Library

be shunted into the goods sheds, unloaded and the goods placed on the correct outgoing dray according to the delivery route. When a carter returned from a collection or delivery run he would almost immediately collect a full dray and go off on another delivery round. As the drays were simple platform vehicles it was easy for the carter to look around the dray to find the goods for any particular delivery.

In the 1920s there were no petrol-engined vehicles that were really suitable for this 'smalls' operation involving the rapid exchange of empty and loaded drays, so the job was left to the horses, although alternative methods were considered. One of the main problems was the restricted spaces, certainly in towns, where the sheer manoeuvrability of horse and dray was unsurpassed. No suitable replacement vehicle was available until 1932 and the advent of the Mechanical Horse. However, experiments were made with 'swap body' or demountable body operation, whereby each lorry had two separate bodies. One body would be stood at the depot being loaded, while the second body was out on the delivery run. Two main schemes were tried: first individual demountable bodies which stood on their own legs and, second, bodies which could transfer by rollers from the lorry chassis on to a loading bay or on to a superannuated horse dray that could stand against a loading bay. The Midland Railway had some electric trucks fitted with a cantilever frame that enabled the body to be demounted and to stand on its own legs. The LMSR and GWR experimented with a great variety of demountable bodies, but

none of the systems were totally safe to use under the conditions found in goods yards at the time, nor were the systems flexible enough to cater for changes in flows of traffic. It is interesting to note that demountable bodies are in vogue in the 1980s.

The railway company vehicle purchasing policies are of interest. Often a local manufacturer would be favoured — LMSR with Karrier and Albion; Southern and Great Western with Thornycroft — but, more importantly, following the purchase of a large number of Ford vehicles, a 'Buy British' campaign was started. Benefitting from this policy, Morris Commercial, Commer, Dennis and to some extent Burford vehicles — although not entirely British — were purchased for the lighter requirements. At the heavier end of the market it was generally Albion, Karrier and Thornycroft which were favoured. Only occasionally were Leyland vehicles purchased although a substantial fleet of Leylands entered the LMSR fleet from the Lancashire & Yorkshire Railway.

Wherever possible the railway companies insisted on buying just the basic chassis and fitting their own standard cab and body, generally in the interest of economy rather than aesthetics. These bodies and cabs were generally built in the railway workshops. There were, of course, always exceptions, such as a large fleet of Dennis 30/45cwt trucks with manufacturer's cabs supplied to the LMSR In the late 1930s.

Although the railway-built cabs were of a standard design for each railway they were often altered to suit different makes of

chassis and special loads. This policy of body and cab building was continued up to the time when manufacturers could offer pressed steel cabs that were less expensive than coach-built railway cabs, or when orders for vehicles outstripped railway workshop production capacity.

One of the more innovative goods distribution schemes to really get of the ground was the 'Railhead Distribution Service'. This simply meant that manufacturers could deliver goods in bulk by rail to a main railway depot or warehouse, and railway staff would ensure that individual orders could be made up and delivered next day direct from the depot. Where sufficient regular traffic was available, vehicles working on these contracts could be supplied in the manufacturers' colours.

As can probably be imagined, during the interwar period nearly every railway station operated a number of delivery vehicles, with each station or depot covering a very small delivery area. This entailed a vast fleet of rail wagons trundling partly full between numerous destinations while 'trunking' the goods. There were over 3,000 depots involved in handling smalls traffic and there were potential delays to goods on any journey, except perhaps those to and from London, and certain large cities.

It was not until the 1930s that large scale schemes were introduced under which less than wagon load traffic was concentrated at railheads for delivery rather than being spread thinly through numerous small depots. These schemes reduced the amount of handling of goods and cut out a large

Above:
The advent of mass production in the 1930s led to the railways purchasing vehicles from large manufacturers, and Morris was proud of an early order for 100 various models from the LNER. These two 1932 Courier four-tonners, for service in London, display the original LNER chronological fleet numbering, soon to be replaced by the more complicated type and capacity numbering system. *Ian Allan Library*

Below:
By the mid-1930s large numbers of the ex-War Department AEC Y type purchased 10 or more years earlier had been updated. As this photograph shows, pneumatic tyres, electric lighting and a modernised cab with windscreen had been fitted. Some of the fleet also had AEC engines replacing the original Tylor engines. Fleet No 877B is shown here at St Pancras. *Ian Allan Library*

Above right:
A Karrier two-tonner seen loading at Abergele in 1934. Although fitted with pneumatic tyres, oil lamps were still in use and the driver had to use the nearside door. The load is typical of the various miscellaneous items carried on collection or delivery work, and note the barrel ramps for unloading heavy items, hanging beside the chassis frame.
Real Photographs

Above:
These Thornycroft Handy two-ton vans, seen at Bricklayers Arms depot in 1934, were part of the small SR fleet.
Ian Allan Library

Left:
The cartage fleet was not comprised of all large vehicles, as all the companies ran a few lightweight vans, including the GWR with this Swindon-built body on a standard Morris Commercial one-ton chassis. Photographed in 1928 at Swindon, the vehicle looks very smart in the brown and cream livery.
Quainton Railway Society

Right:
At least two Albion 30/35cwt trucks were purchased by the LNER in 1932, featuring a special railway design for the road wheels. They are seen here at High Street goods station, Glasgow.
Ian Allan Library

Below:
The SR had several Thornycroft heavy vehicles in its fleet, such as this seven-ton Trusty model capable of hauling a drawbar trailer. This 1937 vehicle appears to have a Thornycroft-built cab.
National Railway Museum

Right:
In the mid and late 1930s the LMSR took delivery of a large number of Dennis Ace vehicles complete with Dennis built cabs. Two models were purchased: a 30cwt model with single rear tyres; and a three-tonner with twin rear tyres as shown here at Wicker goods yard, Sheffield when brand new in 1938. There was also a six-ton version for use with Scammell semi-trailers.
Real Photographs

Above:
A Fordson 7V platform truck fitted with a GWR standard cab. It is a pity that the designers failed to blend the Fordson standard bulbous steel bonnet with their straight cab panels. This vehicle was one of the first 15 to be fitted with the new style cab in 1939 and the design lasted until 1949.
Quainton Railway Society

Below:
The advent of World War 2 meant a stay of execution for many elder members of the railway companies fleets. This Albion model LB35 five-ton overtype had just been overhauled at the LMSR works at Wolverton and put into wartime livery which involved painting all corners white to show up in the blackout and the masked headlamps gave virtually no illumination. It is interesting to note that a nearside rear view mirror had been fitted, although this was not a legal requirement.
National Railway Museum

Above:
Another wartime photograph, showing a Dennis 10-ton six-wheeled petrol engined lorry of 1933 which has been modified to run on gas produced from anthracite burned in the trailer. Since the engine only produced 85hp on petrol and the gas was less powerful, it is safe to assume this converted lorry won no prizes for acceleration!
National Railway Museum

Below:
In 1946 the GWR took delivery of this Dennis Jubilant six-wheel dropside lorry having a reinforced hardwood floor for 12-ton loads. These vehicles were normally fitted with the Dennis 06 diesel engine and the lorry looks completely different from the earlier Dennis supplied to the LMSR.
Ian Allan Library

Four Ford vehicles are shown here in the late 1940s, all based at York. The two bonneted vehicles are Ford BB 2/3 tonners with fleet No FE4180 (new in 1934) still showing the remains of its wartime livery. The six-wheelers are both double-drive Ford Sussex models. FA7100 (new in 1940) is based on a Ford 7V chassis, but is fitted with the optional 24hp four-cylinder engine rather than the more normal 30hp V8 engine; the cab and body were built by Northern Coachbuilders. The other six-wheeler (FN6102 from 1937) used the Ford BBE chassis, but in both cases the extra axle was fitted by County Commercial Cars. *HS Transport Collection*

Left:
With the shortage of vehicles following the end of the war and the Nationalisation of the railways, many different types of lorries were to be found in the railway companies' fleets. Here a Vulcan six-ton flat-bed lorry of the Western Region is unloading a Type A container to a city warehouse. Note the dent in the front of the offside rear wing. *Ian Allan Library*

Right:
A 1952 Morris Commercial FV5 allocated to the Western Region. Originally introduced in 1949 with a Saurer diesel engine, the model was later fitted with a Nuffield diesel. The body design is quite common, featuring a half tilt and hinged flaps in the front of the body to enable long loads to be carried.
National Railway Museum

Below:
The Ford Thames 500E series vehicles were purchased in large numbers by BR in the 1950s and used by all departments from Civil Engineers to Express Parcels with bodies ranging from tippers to vans. Powered by the Ford four-cylinder diesel engine, the standard Briggs cab and bonnet was supplied. Some models, like the one depicted, had rubber wings to reduce maintenance costs.
Colin Green

Left:
In 1962, Proctor & Gamble Ltd required to transport quantities of starch on a regular basis between Glasgow and Birmingham. British Rail received the contract and used a tank-type container, which when on the road was carried on this Albion Reiver fitted with a compressor to pressurise the container for unloading.
R. N. Hannay Collection

During the late 1950s the Ford Motor Co introduced a normal control version of its Thames Trader model. The four-tonner shown here at York featured 16in wheels to give a low loading height. The cab will seat three.
HS Transport Collection

Left:
Driver safety was the thinking behind the 'threepenny-bit' cab design of the British Motor Corporation (BMC) FG series. With angled doors the driver could leave and enter the cab without the door obstructing traffic; also the driver was partially protected by the body. Used mainly for crewbus or vans, this platform truck was one of a small order built in Temple Mills workshops of Eastern Region. *Colin Green*

2
Rural Goods Services

In certain country areas the introduction of metalled roads allowed better access into rural districts and this, plus the reliability of motor vehicles, gave farmers the ability to purchase goods from suppliers further afield and in turn offered wider markets for the farmers' produce. In many areas the railways rapidly became the main carriers of seeds, fertilisers and animal foods to the agricultural community. By establishing warehousing operations at a number of goods depots the railways could offer facilities for receiving products in bulk by rail from manufacturers. The goods would then be stored and distributed as required to farmers and merchants. Invariably the goods depot managers would work closely with the manufacturers' local agents to ensure that the customers received an excellent service, and the manufacturers knew exactly what goods had been despatched daily.

It was not only the manufacturers and customers that benefited from this service,

for the railway companies gained increased productivity from their rail fleet. Previously they had to wait for a private haulier or the farmer's horse and cart to unload the incoming rail wagons. Now with the railway managers in charge the wagons could be unloaded immediately, the goods placed in store or sent out for delivery, and the rail wagons returned for further loads.

Despite the obvious success of these operations and the ability of the vehicles to collect goods for despatch elsewhere while on their rounds, a lot of local traffic could not, by law, be carried by the railways' vehicles. A number of restrictions had been placed on the operation of railway road vehicles by parliamentary statute, especially the clause that all goods had, at some point on their journey, to be carried by rail — the road vehicles were to be used only as 'feeders' to the railway. For some time the railways petitioned against these operational restrictions and eventually in 1928 an Act of Parliament was passed

Right:
To state that this photograph typifies the country lorry service does not do justice to the scene of a World War 1 ex-War Department AEC Y type lorry unloading at a farm near Albrighton in 1929. Under the 1930 Road Traffic Act vehicles running on solid tyres were discriminated against and this led to the conversion of a great number of the older vehicles to pneumatic tyres.
Quainton Railway Society

Left:
In certain rural areas the railway companies were contracted to collect milk from farms within a specified area. Based at Shrivenham in 1929, this Associated Daimler (ADC) 4/5 ton platform lorry with Swindon-built bodywork is operating on a churn collection service within a seven-mile radius from base.
Quainton Railway Society

Below:
Always willing to try out new ideas, the GWR experimented with driver aids for loading milk churns from ground level. The Thornycroft PB four-ton lorry was based at Bewdley when the photograph was taken in 1929 and used on the country lorry services as depicted on the enamelled plate. *Ian Allan Library*

enabling the railways to carry goods throughout by road.

Almost immediately, all companies commenced marketing 'Country Lorry Services'. A number of salesmen promoted the service and ensured it ran smoothly, for the railways could now act as local carriers to the agricultural community. Vehicles would set out to deliver goods immediately they had arrived by rail and collect goods on the journey for local delivery or further afield by rail.

With the ability of the railways to transport freight across the country rapidly, a number of products such as seasonal flowers, horticultural goods and salad crops were moved, often by passenger train, between producing and consuming areas. The close contact between the railway staff and the agricultural community as a whole also gave the railways the opportunity to quote for the bulk flows of traffic at harvest time, such as sugar beet and other root crops.

A further service offered to the farmers was the hiring of hessian sacks. Many milions of sacks were on hire at any one time: for example, the LNER had 3.5 million sacks in circulation in the late 1940s. The lack of control over the final destination of the sacks, however, meant there was little, if any, profit in the operation. In addition, the trend towards bulk movements of grain and seed, and the introduction of expendable plastic sacks, ensured the rapid closure of this operation.

In addition to carrying the more normal seeds and fertilisers, the railway companies had a number of contracts to collect milk from farms. This involved a fleet of platform trucks collecting milk churns, generally within a radius of 7-10 miles of railway stations. The milk would then be delivered to a local dairy for processing. A small number of mechanical aids were used to assist the vehicle driver in loading the churns from ground level.

The railway companies, especially the

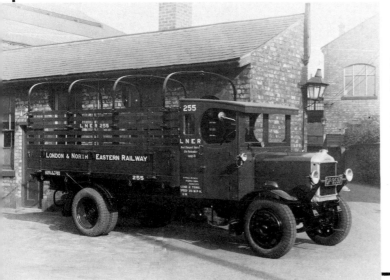

Above:
This five-ton Karrier lorry is working at the start of the SR 'Door-to-Door' country lorry service from Horsham, Sussex in July 1929. It is handling a typical load which at 5-6 miles from the railhead was charged at £2 per ton for a four-ton load. *Ian Allan Library*

Left:
A 1931 Karrier normal control lorry with removable side rails and hoops operated by the LNER at Pickering. It is a large vehicle for only a two-ton load. *HS Transport Collection*

Great Western and Southern, also had contracts involving the bulk transport of milk from a central point such as a country dairy to the large cities, especially London. In a number of cases both terminals were rail connected, but where a road journey was involved, a fleet of four- and six-wheeled road/rail tankers were used, these being transported by rail on flat wagons and hauled on the road by drawbar tractors.

A far more difficult traffic to handle was livestock on the hoof. Numerous rules and restrictions governed the movement of animals, but as the only nationwide carrier the railways were forced to operate fairly large fleets of cattle lorries and rail wagons. Some of the road vehicles had permanent livestock-carrying bodies, while others used a demountable body that would fit on a normal platform truck or trailer. There were also a number of trailers permanently fitted with livestock bodies. As well as moving stock, the railways could undertake to move complete farms from one end of the country to the other.

Following on from the contacts with agricultural merchants and suppliers, the railways became the recognised medium for moving complete agricultural shows around the country during the summer season, supplying fleets of containers, wagons, cranes and staff to help move the show stands. Often, given normal British summers, they would be called upon to supply wooden sleepers to make up roadways through the mud!

Until the early 1950s, British Railways accepted that it was carrier to the agricultural community. However, a decision was made to cease carrying livestock, and therefore livestock facilities at stations were closed down. During the following decade, more and more traffic was given to road hauliers as local goods depots were closed and Dr Beeching, followed by the 1968 Transport Act, finally killed the agricultural service.

Below left:
This Ford model B of 1932 was allocated to the country service of the LNER in the north of England, but was lost in a fire in November 1948.
HS Transport Collection

Above:
In the mid-1930s the SR operated several Bedford WLG two-ton lorries. Note the cast 'Southern Railway' plate on the radiator grille.
Peter Daniels Moto'graphs Collection

Below:
This 1932 Albion lorry carried a load of 45cwt and was based at Hexham. It cost £378 when new and was scrapped in June 1950. *HS Transport Collection*

Right:
A classic six-ton AEC Monarch pictured at York when new in 1932. Fitted with slatted sides above the normal dropside, this vehicle would be used on country services in the North Eastern Region. *HS Transport-Collection*

Below right:
Used for milk collection in the mid-1930s, this Morris Commercial six-tonner has a double deck body and a 'self loading device' to lift the churns from the ground. A total of 135 eight-gal churns could be carried on this 1932 vehicle. *Quainton Railway Society*

Below:
Ford chassis featured strongly in the railway company fleets as they were relatively cheap to buy and run. One of the rarer Ford models was this BB type two-tonner, dating from 1935, converted to forward control. Based at Hitchin and Brimsdown, the vehicle, with railway style cab, had a Westmorland-built body and served for 12 years.
HS Transport Collection

Small vans were also part of the country or rural fleet, like this 1933 Austin 10cwt van based on the 12hp car chassis and with the same engine.
HS Transport Collection

In the later years of country services operation, articulated vehicles became common. This photograph shows a Karrier Bantam three-ton unit in 1946.
HS Transport Collection

Above:
An early 1930s horsebox for the LNER on a Leyland Cub chassis. *Ian Allan Library*

Below right:
One of two Leyland Cub horseboxes with Vincent bodies supplied to the LMSR in 1934. *Ian Allan Library*

Facing page, top:
The LNER found that its horsebox fleet needed additional vehicles in 1938. As a result some Albion Valkyrie coach chassis were purchased and fitted with Harrington bodies. The vehicles were used mainly in the North Yorkshire area and are seen here loading at a trainer's premises.
W. J. Aldridge Collection

Facing page, bottom:
The Harrington body was so successful that further examples were purchased after the war by both the LNER and the SR. The Maudslay Marathon II coach chassis was originally fitted with a six- cylinder, 7,400cc petrol engine but it is thought that the vehicles were re-engined with AEC diesels at a later date. They were the pride of the fleet and the prototype for a popular model in the Dinky Supertoy range. *HS Transport Collection*

41

Above:
This is one of the SR's version of the same vehicle resplendent in dark green livery with black mud-guards and gilt lettering lined out in black. These were urgently needed by the SR as all its horseboxes had been destroyed in an air raid. The new vehicles could carry three horses, with their grooms (who had a bell communication with the driver), plus all the necessary fodder and equipment. The overall length of the vehicle was 25ft 5in (21ft for the actual body), with a height of 11ft and an unladen weight of six-ton 17¾ cwt.
Ian Allan Library

Below:
The movement of livestock was a lucrative traffic for the GWR and in 1930 it had a special double-deck body constructed on a Maudslay ML 3 4/5-ton chassis which had previously been a bus. When not required for small animals the upper deck was removable for the carriage of cattle.
Peter Daniels Moto'graphs Collection

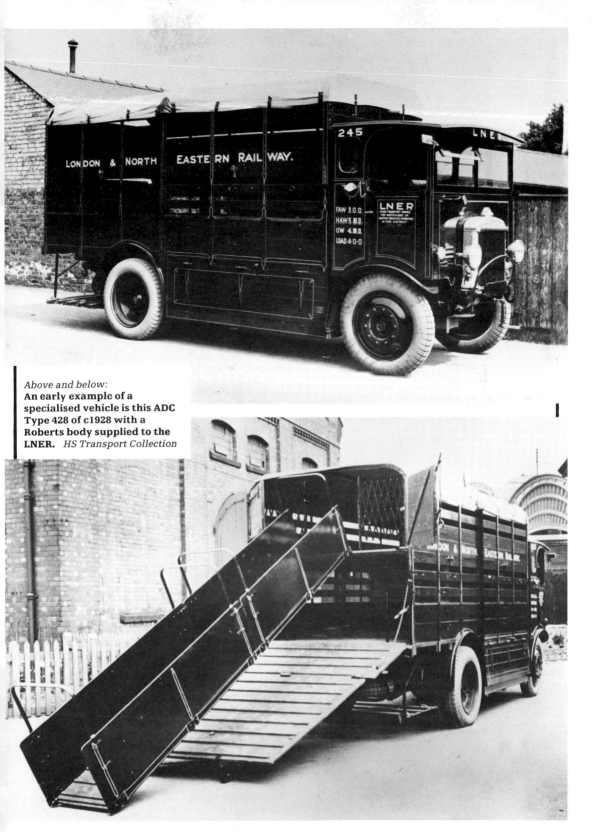

Above and below:
An early example of a specialised vehicle is this ADC Type 428 of c1928 with a Roberts body supplied to the LNER. *HS Transport Collection*

Above:
In 1932 the LMSR operated this Fordson Type B which had been converted by County Commercial Cars to a double drive six-wheeler capable of carrying three tons. Known as the Ford Sussex, this one carried a special livestock body. *Real Photographs*

Below:
This Fordson conversion was allocated to work in one of the joint LMSR and GWR areas from 1936 onwards.
Quainton Railway Society

Above:

This ubiquitous Bedford, new to the LNER in 1936, carried a demountable body for the carriage of livestock. When the body was lifted off the vehicle it became a normal three-ton flat truck.
HS Transport Collection

Left:

A Thornycroft Sturdy with cattle truck body purchased by the GWR just prior to the war. It is shown here in wartime livery.
Peter Daniels Moto'graphs Collection

Below left:

A later type of demountable body built by Penman Engineering of Dumfries on an Albion FT series chassis dating from 1948 and operated by BR Scottish Region.
Penman Engineering

4

Parcels Vans

By the 1860s the railway companies could offer an extensive, and often competing, network of lines and stations covering the whole of the country. As well as being able to handle goods traffic in rail wagons there was the additional carrying capacity available in the brake vans on passenger trains. This capacity was used initially for passengers' hand luggage but was soon made available for 'luggage in advance' traffic. This operation relied on the customer bringing his luggage to the station and arranging collection at the destination.

Developing this idea, the railways companies sold an express parcels service to industry, utilising the passenger train service to move the parcels rapidly across the country.

Some of the more enterprising railways quickly arranged parcels collection and delivery services. This service was often included in the carriage charge, but where the journey was outside established boundaries an excess charge may have been made. Originally, hand-carts were used on this operation and were restricted to a radius of half-a-mile from the station. As the traffic increased, a fleet of horse vans was gradually introduced operating over greater distances. Concurrent with this change was the introduction of a single rate to include collection, movement and delivery where previously three separate charges had been raised.

Since all the traffic concerned was carried on passenger trains, and received a higher

Left:
A 1926 photograph of a 30cwt Burford van with simple but heavy van body built at Swindon (fleet No 578). Note the primitive weatherproofing for the driver.
Quainton Railway Society

Above right:
A Fordson B type of 1933 with LNER standard type of body, including a steeply sloping Luton head to the 2½-ton van.
HS Transport Collection

Right:
A Guy two-ton forward control chassis with a Swindon-built van body, registered GJ 2317 in 1931. The products of Guy Motors were rarely purchased by the railway companies.
Real Photographs

level of service than that offered by the more humble goods train, higher rates were charged. This resulted in a fleet of vehicles, both horse-drawn and eventually mechanised, that was given a different livery from the cartage vehicles. The vehicles tended to be lettered 'Express Parcels', featured lining-out, shaded lettering and often a more elaborate colour scheme. There was a further variation in that the majority of express parcels vans were smaller in size than other members of the railway van fleet. Because the carriage charges were higher and the parcel size was

Above:

In the mid-1930s the SR took delivery of a few of the popular Bedford type BYC 12cwt vans for light duties.

Peter Daniels Moto'graphs Collection

Right:

In the mid-1930s the LNER too was using small vans for urgent deliveries, in this case, Morris 10cwt vehicles, with their own bodies. Also shown is a one-ton Ford Type B. The steep rake of the Luton roof is very noticeable.

HS Transport Collection

Below right:

A close view of one of the LNER Morris 10cwt vans.

A. P. Sposito

Far right:

A large number of Dennis Ace Type 96 two-ton vans were used by the LMSR, and those shown here are part of one order for 29 delivered in 1934. With gold leaf and lining out on the crimson and black livery, these vans were particularly smart and ideal for the express parcels traffic. There was direct access from the cab to the body, the interior headroom was 6ft allowing a man to stand upright, and often carried a van boy who would sort parcels for the next stop. *Ian Allan Library*

smaller, the same amount of revenue could be obtained with a small parcels van as with a larger general goods vehicle.

From an operational point of view, in the urban areas express parcels vans were run as a separate fleet since they could operate to capacity at most times and were run directly from the passenger stations. In the more rural areas, cartage traffic and express parcels would be handled on the same delivery vehicles.

It is amusing to consider that throughout the early history of express rail parcels it was quite common for a next day delivery service to be offered from the provinces into London. We consider that the current influx of guaranteed next-day delivery services offered by road hauliers is something new. In fact, the railways gave a similar service over 50 years ago and were often using horse vans for delivery!

Mechanisation of the express parcels fleet was a little later than that of the rural goods delivery service, but ahead of the town cartage fleets, as the horse and van were ideally suited to short journey stop-start work. Nevertheless, a number of lightweight vans were in use by the mid-1920s for parcel deliveries. Prominent among these were Model T Fords, Burford and Thornycrofts. The introduction of mass produced vehicles by Ford and Morris Commercial led to large fleets of these motors being purchased. As traffic increased, so a number of heavier vans were obtained, utilising the same chassis as their goods-carrying brothers. Almost every van featured a poster space on the van side for advertising various railway services.

Although the basis of the parcels delivery fleet was petrol-engined vehicles, there were always small numbers of electric vehicles, and these are covered in a later chapter.

Development of the parcels vans, before and after World War 2, mirrored that of the goods vehicle fleet, with further mass produced vehicles purchased when suitable and available. By the time of Nationalisation, a very varied fleet was operated. British Railways, however, wanted to standardise the fleet and had evolved a set of standards as follows: covered vans of one-, two- and three-ton capacity, with a small turning circle, high bulk capacity, low unladen weight to allow maximum use of the 30mph limit, plus easy to maintain bodywork. As a result, large numbers of Karrrier Bantams, Austins, Morris Commercials and Ford Thames vans entered the fleet.

To some extent the parcels delivery market was even more competitive than the general goods market. Although some of the competition had been stifled by the 1933 licensing regulations, and the takeover of Pickfords and Carter Paterson in the same year, there still remained a large number of local express parcel carriers. Most of these had reciprocal agreements with other local carriers to offer a nationwide express delivery service in direct competition to the railway owned or operated companies. In addition there were 'directional carriers'

Above:
When Ford introduced its Thames range of two-, three-, four- and five-ton vans in 1949/50 they were purchased in large numbers by BR, the two- and three-ton versions having van bodies, the difference in the two types being the length of the rear overhang, with larger section tyres and servo-assisted brakes being fitted to the higher capacity model. Rubber wings were fitted to some of the vehicles, which saved on maintenance costs but looked untidy. *F. Cassell*

Below:
The Morris Commercial equivalent to the Ford Thames was the LC5 three-ton model. Again featuring an integral cab, this particular vehicle does not look properly dressed without the advertisement on the rear panel. *F. Cassell*

Left:
The successor to the Commer Q25 model was the 1¼-ton van of 1957 which had a Karrier-style front. Although some vans were supplied complete, most regions purchased a chassis/scuttle unit and then built their own parcels van body. Temple Mills (ER) built the body for this LMR van, seen at Leicester. *F. Cassell*

Below:
Karrier Bantams continued to be supplied in many guises. This van was one of 200 built at Temple Mills in 1961/62 and had sliding doors which contained a 'drop section' that fell in the space between the front mudguard and the front panel. These short wheelbase Karriers were ideal for town and city deliveries. *F. Cassell*

In 1924 the GWR canvassed some of its best and regular customers which were using the railway vans for collection and delivery work, to ascertain whether they would be prepared to pay a little more and have the vehicle painted and lettered in their own livery. The result was that the GWR ran a fleet of contract hire vans and secured some long-term contracts, and by 1928 over 30 vehicles were in the customers' own liveries.

The vehicles were maintained and driven by railway employees, often in the customer's uniform, and to all intents and purposes they gave the impression that the vehicles, mostly vans, were the property of the supplier or the manufacturer of the goods carried. Thus the firm concerned had the advantage of the advertising value and prestige of its own fleet without the worries of the maintenance, administration and staffing.

Top:
The LNER supplied this Albion for Kemps Bisuits in 1931. The vehicle was used as an ambulance during the war and was finally scrapped in 1949.
HS Transport Collection

Right:
Another GWR-owned Dennis 50cwt van, also in the livery of Kemps Biscuits.
Quainton Railway Society

Above right:
In the mid-1930s Worcester-based Hill, Evans & Co relied on this GWR-owned Morris Commercial van to handle its products.
Quainton Railway Society

In 1936 at least three two-ton Morris Commercial vans like this were used, with other vehicles, for Rowntree products in the GWR area.
Real Photographs

Right:
The sides of this two-ton Morris Commercial van, owned by the GWR, were of highly polished metal — a fashion started about 1937.
Quainton Railway Society

Below right:
The GWR still had the Macfarlane Lang contract in 1939 when this Morris two-ton van was supplied.
Quainton Railway Society

Bottom right:
British Rail inherited and still held the Cadbury contract, supplying this BMC Type FG van for the purpose.
W. Aldridge Collection

6

Mechanical Horses

Mechanisation of part of the cartage fleet took place during the 1920s with petrol engined vehicles replacing the horse and cart from certain operations. However, the majority of the new vehicles were purchased to operate new services that were introduced to meet customer demand. There was, however, one specific operation which remained obstinately with the horse and dray. The operation in question was the town cartage of less than wagon load traffic. The volume of traffic precluded the use of small vans like the express parcels operation, yet it was town deliveries that presented the worst access problems and the constant stop-start, short mileage operation that was ideally suited to horse and dray work. With the low mileage involved, two or three delivery runs could be completed each day and all the horse needed to do was drop an empty dray at the depot and collect a loaded dray. This was literally a moment's job and no petrol-engined vehicle at the time could offer the total flexibility required.

The railway managements had considered this problem for some time and had introduced a number of demountable bodies on to standard lorry chassis. Unfortunately the transfer of full and empty bodies was neither simple nor safe and the three-ton to five-ton vehicles used in these experiments were no match for the horse and dray in manoeuvrability.

In 1929 the LMSR Road Motor Engineers instigated a series of experiments at Wolverton. They outlined plans for a small articulated vehicle to replace the horse and dray; articulation was necessary both to ensure small turning circles and allow simple exchange of trailers. Initial trials used a converted Morris Cowley car and modified horse dray; later, a three-wheeled electric platform truck was used in conjunction with a similar dray. This second experiment emphasised the need for

Right:
The first trial of a mechanical horse occured on 3 December 1930 in Camden Goods yard. The LMS and Karrier Motors co-operated in the joint venture which resulted in production of the Karrier Cob. In this photograph the prime mover is about to reverse under the horse dray, when the jaws will fit under the dray axle. The second man then rocks the lever to and fro, thus pumping up the hydraulic cylinder which will lift the front wheels of the dray clear of the ground. *Ian Allan Library*

Left:
A very early model of the Karrier Cob in service.
Ian Allan Library

Below:
Further development of the Karrier Cob followed the company's take-over by the Rootes Group and its move to a new factory at Luton. A new cab was fitted and the engine became a Rootes product in place of the early Jowett engine; the 'J' coupling was now a production option. These vehicles for the LNER were new in 1936, shown here at King's Cross where the ability to turn at 90° is clearly seen. Prior to this the LMSR and SR had taken delivery of a batch in 1934 and the GWR had 15 in 1938. *P. Newman*

Right:
A close-up view of an LMSR Karrier Cob in wartime livery.
P. Newman

a three-wheel tug unit in conjunction with a short wheelbase semi-trailer. In fact, with a single front wheel capable of turning through an 180° arc, the vehicle proved itself capable of doing all that could be done by a horse drawn vehicle.

Conveniently for the railways, the Karrier Motor Co in Huddersfield had just introduced its Colt model. This was a small, narrow three-wheeled chassis designed for dust-cart use. At the request of the LMSR engineers, a tractor version of the Colt was built and called the Cob. This vehicle was fitted with a Jowett 7hp two-cylinder horizontally-opposed water-cooled engine, chain-drive reduction gear and three-speed gearbox. It fulfilled the railway's needs as far as manoeuvrability was concerned, but the coupling of tractor to trailer, in the initial stages, left a lot to be desired.

The prototype and early production Cobs used a coupling device that gripped the horse dray's front axle and lifted it clear of the ground. Since this required hand operation, it could hardly be called an instantaneous coupling. In addition the horse drays that were used would not stand up to the faster speeds generated by the Karrier tractor. However, further

development by the LMSR brought the 'Wolverton coupling' into use. This was essentially a pair of inclined channels on the tractor, working in conjunction with small jockey wheels on a trailer designed for mechanical haulage. The first demonstration of the Karrier Cob was at Maiden Lane (LMSR) depot in London on 18 September 1930 and the first press viewing on 3 November 1930.

Meanwhile, the Napier Aero Engine Co had, quite independently, realised a need for a vehicle suitable for town cartage work. The company designed a vehicle from the ground up, incorporating single front wheel steering and a side-valve four-cylinder petrol engine. When two or three prototypes had been built, the whole project was sold to Scammell Lorries of Watford, which rapidly patented the idea. This particular vehicle was called the 'Mechanical Horse' and featured an almost foolproof system of instantly coupling tractor to trailer that is still in use today. This model was purchased in great numbers by all the railway companies and was very successful in replacing the horse on town cartage work.

Over in Huddersfield, Karrier improved its Cob model with a larger engine and

Below:

The six-ton Scammell MH was similar to the three-ton version, but featured a 2,000cc engine, uprated axle, larger rear tyres and larger coupling gear. The three-ton and six-ton trailers were not interchangeable, but to add confusion some six-ton trailers were fitted with three-ton coupling gear and some three-ton Mechanical Horses received six-tonner engines for special jobs. The SR model shown here is standard.
National Railway Museum

Right:

An ex-LMSR Scammell MH6 renumbered into ER fleet numbering (Sc) series, in BR colours of maroon and cream. It is loading a trailer with container on the motor vessel *Caledonian Princess* on its maiden voyage from Stranrear to Larne on 16 December 1961.
Ian Allan Library

remained about 25 miles per day. The Scarab six-tonner continued to be built until 1967, but the three-tonner was replaced in 1964 by the Townsman. Again a three-wheeler, the Townsman was built using a fibreglass cab (built at Thornycroft's works in Basingstoke) and fitted with a Standard diesel engine rather than a Perkins engine. This model, designed specially for British Railways, remained in production until 1967, when impending changes in road transport Construction & Use regulations appeared to rule out the continuing use of non-braked single-steering road wheels. Since neither British Railways nor Scammell wished to be involved in a complete re-design of the vehicle, production of three-wheelers was halted from 1968. In their place came four-wheel tractor units in the shape of the Ford D series and Karrier Bantams. The D series was rated for a nominal five-ton payload although the majority of the three-wheelers replaced were three-tonners. The six-ton Scammells had been used mainly on freight duties as opposed to the town cartage origin of the three-tonners.

By the mid-1980s the D series automatic coupling tractors were themselves phased out of service as the need for instant turn-round of vehicles had long since departed. The delivery operation was now based in a small number of large depots with full-day journeys for most vehicles. As a result, a rigid van would suffice, therefore ending a 53-year-old association with automatic trailer couplings.

As a sideline it should be mentioned that a 'Light Mechanical Horse' was also designed and at least a couple of prototypes built around 1934. Looking similar to the standard Scammell Mechanical Horse, the light version could only carry 30cwt. The engine was an air-cooled V twin of 832cc developing 15bhp. The small engine was used to prove a theory that larger engines were unnecessary on local work, but this was incorrect. The model was not a success and full production was never commenced.

Left:
The Scammell MH series was replaced by the Scamell Scarab in 1948 and both three-ton and six-ton versions were produced. The Scarab had an all-metal cab and mechanically was different from its predecessor by having the engine set low behind the cab, and this incorporated the gearbox and rear axle. Two ER three-tonners are shown here, LUV 21 with the normal production cab and KXY 186 which had a wooden cab built by BR at Temple Mills and was one of about 100 so equipped. Both vehicles spent their working lives in London and were withdrawn in 1965 and 1964 respectively.
HS Transport Collection

Left:
A three-ton Scarab with a typical day's load. The grille behind the driver's door is the air intake for the radiator which is situated in the rear wall of the cab. *Hub Publishing*

Bottom left:
Regular servicing and preventative maintenance were very important in a fleet of any size. In the case of three-wheelers special facilities were required since they could not run on to a normal pit! At King's Cross in 1957 the Scarabs were serviced over a special 50ft-long pit allowing easy access to the low slung engine and gearbox.
Ian Allan Library

Above right:
In 1965 the Townsman replaced the Scarab. BR ordered 1,290 of these new units which had a glass-fibre cab and a number of new design and mechanical features. *Ian Allan Library*

Right:
The final livery for the mechanical horse fleet was the Railfreight one in a 'stone shade of yellow'. This illustration was taken in 1961, with a standard BR Mk 3 van.
Ian Allan Library

7
Articulated Four-Wheel Tractor Units

Various forms of articulated road vehicles have been used by the railways following the GWR's introduction of an American Knox seven-ton tractor unit in 1918. Like all contemporary articulated units, it suffered from a very cumbersome coupling operation and tractor and trailer were not easily separated. There were no such items as fifth-wheel couplings, lead-on ramps or wind-up landing legs. All trailers required manual jacking and the tractor had to be reversed exactly under the turntable or coupling was impossible.

Perhaps the best known early articulated units were the Scammell heavy duty 15-ton, four-wheel tractors of which the railways had a few, some with flat or sided trailers and others with low bed machinery trailers. There were also a few smaller articulated units in use with the railways, including

Thornycrofts with Carrimore trailers. The biggest selling point of articulation at the time was increased payload at little extra cost.

The introduction in 1932 of the Scammell Automatic Coupling, along with the Mechanical Horse, completely changed everybody's concept of articulation. Here was a foolproof method of exchanging trailers in moments, with none of the previous associated problems. For instance, brakes and lights were connected immediately so there was no fear of the trailer overtaking the tractor on hard braking if the driver had forgotten to connect brake cables.

Initially, automatic couplings were fitted only to three-wheelers, which, due to their lack of speed and stability, were mainly restricted to town work. Vehicles which

Right:
Although this photograph has been published before, it does illustrate the original GWR articulated tractor of 1918 — an American Knox with one of its three trailers that were adapted at Swindon. Note the very basic turntable at the rear of the tractor and the landing legs on the trailer.
Ian Allan Library

covered the more rural duties were generally rigid types, occasionally using drawbar trailers. It was soon realised that more use could be made of automatic coupling trailers behind four-wheel tractors on some of the longer urban duties. As a result, a number of Dennis and Thornycroft nominal three-ton chassis were fitted with six-ton coupling gear almost identical to that on the larger Mechanical Horse. Shortly before the war, Bedford produced a tractor unit suitable for mounting the Scammell coupling gear. This coupling was unique in that it omitted the tractor's rear chassis cross member due to the need for the trailer jockey leg to run between two parallel ramps on top of the tractor chassis. As a result of the success of the first Bedford conversions, the model became a production option rather than a special. Many thousands of Bedford OXC/ Scammell tractor units were produced for the armed forces during the war and these helped to establish articulation.

After the war, Bedford and Scammell jointly marketed the OSS chassis, specifically designed for Scammell coupling gear. These vehicles were even badged Bedford-Scammell and the manufacturer's warranty applied to both tractor and coupling gear. The vehicle was capable of handling an eight-ton load and this particular model was bought in quantities by the railways as well as road hauliers. During the late 1940s and all through the 1950s, virtually every major lorry manufacturer offered Scammell automatic couplings on its vehicles. The booming market brought in a number of imitators, including both Hands and Taskers, but sensibly all trailers remained interchangeable. In fact, railway purchases outran Scammell's production and a number of manufacturers received orders,

Right:
One of two permanently coupled Scammell tractors and 10-ton high-sided trailers, seen in September 1929 leaving the premises of a jam maker at Slough. *Real Photographs*

Below:
In 1930 the LMSR was operating this Scammell articulated unit for transporting machinery and similar loads.
Ian Allan Library

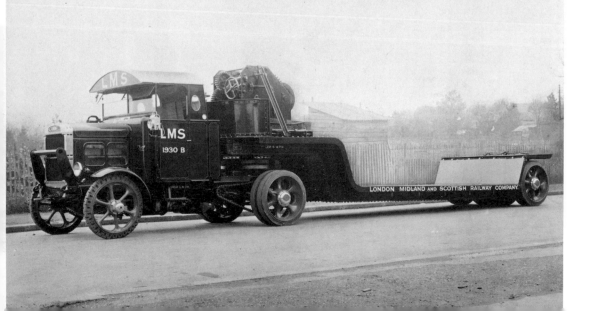

fitting the Scammell trailer parts to their own frames and bodies.

Most of the manufacturers offering articulated versions of their lorries during the period 1938-60 did little more than to build a shorter wheelbase chassis, raise the back axle ratio and alter the carburettor jets. There was very little extra strength built in and the tractor's braking system was not altered. The resulting vehicle was cheap to buy but possibly expensive to run.

Although the six-ton coupling gear was the main seller outside the railways, the three-ton version, mounted on a four-wheel Karrier Bantam chassis, featured in many railway orders from 1945 onwards. In this case it was the Karrier version of the Scammell coupling.

For 20 years after the war the automatic coupling reigned supreme for articulated trucks up to 12-tons capacity. However, the alterations in Construction & Use regulations, from 1964, allowing 32 tons gross on certain articulated vehicles, sounded the death knell for the automatic coupling. Despite the introduction of some larger vehicles, on the whole, the railway fleet did not take immediate advantage of the new gross weights. Where the new regulations were useful was for handling the new ISO standard containers, which were carried by Freightliner trains.

During the 1960s, implementation of the Beeching Plan resulted in the demise of full bulk train load traffic. The less than wagon load traffic which made up the Sundries Division was shortly to pass to the new National Freight Corporation. As a result, after 1970, the only railway-operated articulated vehicles were the 32-ton gross articulated trucks that worked with the Freightliner traffic.

By 1983, virtually all automatic coupling vehicles had disappeared from National

Right:
One of three Thornycroft Bulldog articulated six-wheelers for six-ton payloads, supplied to the LNER in 1934.
Ian Allan Library

Below:
In 1938 the LMSR added to its already large fleet of Dennis Ace machines by purchasing some prime mover units and trailers for six-ton loads.
Ian Allan Library

Above:
The SR's move to articulation was to purchase Thornycroft Nippy tractive units in 1939, again for a six-ton load. *Ian Allan Library*

Below:
The GWR also used Thornycroft Nippy articulated units, but designed its own Swindon safety cabs which were built by Hampshire Car Bodies (HCB), Thornycroft and, in this case, by Whitson. The GWR used its telegraphic codes for most items of equipment — DYAK-AF here — a process which continued for a short time with BR. *Ian Allan Library*

the road/rail tankers. At the most there were only about 120 of these built, to a very high specification, mainly by Dysons of Liverpool. They featured stainless steel tanks and Ackerman steering on the front axle and were constructed to fit within the railway loading gauge when carried on rail flat wagons. Both four- and six-wheeled version were built for carrying products such as beer and milk.

It was also possible for a normal articulated tractor unit fitted with automatic coupling to be modified into a drawbar tractor by the addition of a ballast weight on the coupling gear and a separate hand-operated brake valve to operate the trailer's vacuum brakes.

The policy of purchasing drawbar tractors continued after the war, although not all the manufacturers which had

Above:
Following hard on the heels of Chernard-Walcker was the French owned Latil concern, whose Traulier model tractor was built under licence in the UK by Shelvoke & Drewry. This vehicle was popular as a forestry tractor, having four-wheel drive, four-wheel steering plus a powerful winch. The SR registered this example in June 1935 and it is seen at Nine Elms depot.
Peter Daniels Moto'graphs Collection

Right:
A close-up view of Latil Traulier operated by the LMSR & GWR and purchased in 1936.
Ian Allan Library

supplied vehicles prewar could offer suitable models. The Sandbach-based Fodens Ltd supplied a large number of forestry tractors for the first time, while the French Latil Co offered an updated version of its prewar model. A number of ex-army 4×4 gun tractors were also purchased, along with helpings of new vehicles from Unipower and ERF.

A new design of drawbar tractor was specified by 1960, with a view to large-scale purchases, but the onset of articulation — with possible increases in vehicle size — led to the restriction of the order to just two or three examples. In addition, by the 1960s road hauliers were generally able to handle these smaller outsize loads with ease, and by the end of the decade the era of the railway drawbar tractor had all but disappeared.

The final curtain on pre-Nationalisation drawbar tractors fell in 1980 when a 1946 Foden DG, still in maroon and cream, was withdrawn from use. This vehicle had been stabled with an Emergency Control Train and has since been sold for preservation.

Right:
One of the LMSR-owned Latil's towing a brand new Dyson-built road-rail tanker trailer into the CLC Brunswick Yard in Liverpool. Note how all four wheels of the Latil are steering and also the Ackermann steering on the trailer.
Real Photographs

Below:
In 1930 the Karrier Motor Co introduced its model TT drawbar tractor based on Chernard Walcker principles, which allowed some of the weight on the trailer to be transferred to the tractor, thus increasing adhesion. The tractor is coupled to a six-ton trailer carrying three open H type containers at Hackney Electrical Works.
Stevens-Stratten Collection

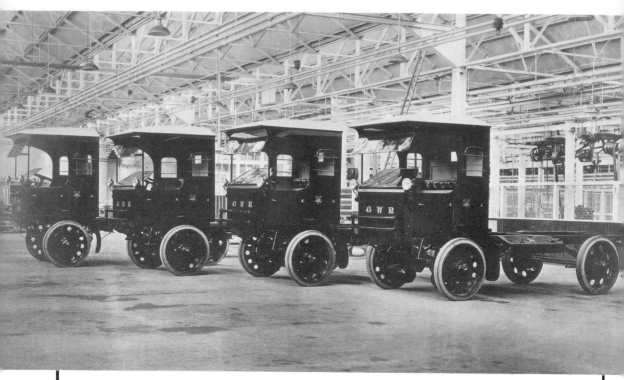

Above:
In 1919/20 the GWR again experimented with battery electric vehicles, purchasing four front-wheel drive 2½-ton models from Ransomes of Ipswich. Swindon works built the cabs and easily removable van bodies for parcels work. The GWR also ordered two 3½-ton and a 1½-ton model from Ransomes.
Ian Allan Library

Right:
After its Ransomes, the GWR did not operate any more battery electric vehicles until 1947 when it took delivery of this standard 25/30cwt Brush-Bred vehicle. *Ian Allan Library*

specific plans were laid to purchase a large fleet of articulated electric trucks and a trial fleet was placed in operation in cities such as Hull, York and Middlesbrough. Had this operation been successful several thousand of these vehicles might have been purchased. This bulk order would have allowed the manufacturers to bring the vehicle price down to around that of the equivalent petrol vehicle. The petrol vehicles however were still cheaper to run than electrics and despite further small scale purchases during the 1950s no further electrics were ordered until the electric vehicle manufacturers could take advantage of modern technology in the late 1970s, by which time railway owned vehicles were on the decrease.

Right:

In September 1949 the LMR of BR took delivery of the first of a new one-ton van from NCB Electric (Smith's Delivery Vehicles Ltd of Gateshead). The chassis was standard apart from 27in by 6in low loading oversize tyres, but the body was specially developed for BR, having a sliding door in the cab giving access to the 330cu ft body. Above the normal rear tailboard was a roller shutter and the front and rear mudguards were rubber. The new vehicles were capable of 18mph and could work 37 miles on a full charge. They were withdrawn after approximately nine years in service. *Ian Allan Library*

Centre right:

A battery-electric mechanical horse was depicted in the chapter dealing with that subject, but in 1952 BR ordered over 100 electric articulated tractors for large scale evaluation purposes. This is a 1952 Morrison Electricar tractor capable of handling a 2½-ton load. The Austin Motor Co acquired a 50% interest in Morrison in 1948, and formed a consortium with Crompton Parkinson to produce the vehicles under the Morrison name and design.
Ian Allan Library

Bottom right:

A prototype Morrison Electricar battery electric articulated tractor Type GT5 seen while on trial in Hull in August 1950. This one-off vehicle survived to become part of the National Railway Museum's road vehicle collection, although by then it had been fitted with a standard production cab.
HS Transport Collection

The introduction of containerised traffic on the railway demanded a rethink on a safe means of transferring the containers from one mode of transport to the other. Until this time loads had been handled by old-fashioned hand-operated yard cranes, either static or mounted on rail wagons. A combination of a fixed, straight jib and low capacity restricted their use to handling empty containers. As a result, a more up-to-date handling system was required.

Within certain large depots, an overhead gantry crane was considered the most suitable, but the high cost of these units ruled out their use in all but the major yards. Instead a fleet of mobile cranes was envisaged, these being able to move between yards to work as required. In fact, mobile crane purchases followed separate paths: either a heavy duty unit, able to travel between sites, or a smaller crane

restricted to working in one locality. Where it was deemed uneconomical to operate mobile cranes then a modernised static yard crane would be used.

In British Railways days, the range of containers became fairly standardised, as detailed below:

Type	Description	Length	Width	Height	Capacity
a	Small covered, end door	7ft	6ft	6ft 6in	3 tons (later 4 tons)
b	Large covered, end and/or side door	14ft	6ft	6ft 6in	4 tons
c	Open small, end door	7ft	6ft	3ft 4in	3-4 tons
d	Open large, side and/or end door	13ft	6ft	3ft 4in	4 tons
h	Open, small shallow sides	7ft	3ft 9in	1ft 6in	3 tons 3cwt

Facing page, bottom:
Delivering carcasses of meat to a retail butcher in the 1930s from a wooden bodied insulated LMSR container.
Stevens-Stratten Collection

Above:
This Karrier GH5 model, with a new LMSR light alloy container, is loading at Salford Museum. For a number of reasons, mainly due to high initial cost, this type of container was never mass produced. The Karrier has been converted to pneumatic tyres and electric lighting but the old style cab remains.
Stevens-Stratten Collection

Right:
One of the many schemes for reducing costs was the GWR's collapsible container. When erected it could carry three tons; but when empty it could be collapsed, taking up little space, and thus could be returned cheaply.
Ian Allan Library

In slightly more detail, individual variations were:

AF: Small, covered, highly insulated for frozen foods, ice cream, etc, using dry ice as a refrigerant and with 9in insulation.
BC: Large, covered, for bicyles.
BD: Large, covered, for general use.
BK: Large, covered, for furniture, removals, rolls of cloth, and hanging garments.
BM: Large, covered, for freshly killed meat, and with roof hooks.
FM: Large, covered, insulated for frozen meat, with 2in insulation and able also to use dry ice as a refrigerant.

In addition there were numbers of bottom discharge containers for limestone, tanks for liquids mounted on container bases, and also glass cradles. All these featured standard fittings to allow easy attachment to road or rail vehicles. Although none of these containers are used by the railways today, one type of container still remains in production. This is the tote bin, a top loading, bottom discharge container used for bulk powder, bulk granules and chemicals. These are generally used by road hauliers who little realise they have to thank the railways for their convenience.

Mention should also be made of the SW container. This was a one-ton capacity small wheeled container which could be pushed inside a rail van or loaded on to a lorry for delivery. It was treated rather like a pallet would be today, but required no mechanised handling such as forklift or pallet trucks.

The modernisation plans of the mid-1950s envisaged a great future for the container. Schemes were in hand to manufacture light alloy five-ton containers, although there were no thoughts on upgrading the existing fleet, except by replacement of life expired containers. The road vehicles of this era could certainly carry a heavier load, as could the rail wagons, and it is surprising that no thought was given at this time to increased payload.

A brave attempt was made by British Railways to upgrade the concept of containerisation by starting a number of timed express services between major conurbations. Perhaps the best known of these was the Condor service offering a next day delivery between London and Glasgow. A competing service was started by a private company trading as Tartan Arrow. The London Midland Region appeared to be the main instigator of new containerised services of which Speedfreight was one. This service used a small number of modern, square sided containers on specific services, but was never universal enough to compete with the road hauliers.

Far left:
In BR days containers were in general circulation rather than belonging to one specific region. Here a 1949 Western Region Thornycroft Nippy is being loaded with a standard BD type container from a BR conflat rail wagon via a Shelvoke & Drewry Freightlifter crane.
Ian Allan Library

Above left:
Prior to the advent of palletisation and shrink-wrapping, most lorry and container loading was done by hand. Without a loading bank, placing four tons of cloth by hand was a tiring and time-consuming job to fill this BD type container when Jacqmar Fashions moved from London to Burnley. The tractor is the ubiquitous Bedford OSS model with a Scammell six-ton 15ft platform trailer.
Ian Allan Library

Left:
An unusual purchase by BR in 1954 was a small number of Sentinel seven-ton flat-bed lorries, which were fitted with the Sentinel four- or six-cylinder underfloor engines. The platform body was made of light alloy and could fit containers between the raves. The container is an AF insulated type.
Ian Allan Library

Right:

In 1958 the Birds Eye Co introduced 100 of these four-ton AFP containers for transporting frozen food from factory to depot. The containers could accept four one-ton pallets and used dry ice to keep the internal temperature at 0°F. The tractor is an Austin WE normal control unit with Scammell coupling gear based at Great Yarmouth. *Ian Allan Library*

Below:

Although the general purpose BD container is no longer in common use the tote bin is still with us. These bins were designed for the carriage of various powder products and feature top loading and bottom discharge. The examples illustrated were photographed at Leamington Spa in 1958 on a Dennis Pax five-ton flat lorry.
Ian Allan Library

Another new project was the 'Bulkrane' concept introduced in 1961 that, thankfully, never got past the prototype stage. The scheme was designed to eliminate the container's biggest drawback, the fact that it needed a crane to transfer a container from road to rail. The Bulkrane, in contrast, had its own loading and unloading device. Based on a Foden eight-wheel chassis fitted with oversize skip loader arms, the vehicle could handle nine types of specialised container. The specification was so comprehensive that the vehicle was even fitted with a compressor to unload bulk containers. A further scheme called 'Leapfrog', also using a Foden eight-wheel chassis, involved a road/rail tank capable of carrying out deliveries to petrol stations. Both these schemes were a little far fetched.

The realities of falling freight revenues in the 1960s led to a number of changes to the whole concept of containerisation. On the one hand Dr Beeching wanted to avoid completely all 'wagon-load traffic', a category into which containers fell. On the other hand, the British Railways Board was preparing to introduce Liner Trains, carrying large containers between about 50 terminals, on timed services. The containers were to be of 8ft by 8ft section with provisional lengths between 10ft and 36ft. Into consideration came also the ISO standard container used by shipping companies. Very soon the Speedfreight and Liner Trains concepts were altered to fit in with the ISO specification and so Freightliners were born. These are trains run to a timetable carrying any company's standard ISO containers. Unfortunately, an inter-union dispute led to a long delay in introducing these services to all-comers. In the meantime, the old containers were rapidly being phased out along with the goods depots and wagon load traffic. By 1968 about 30,000 containers were in use, but by 1979 only about 300 remained, the traffic having moved mainly to road or Freightliner.

This is an almost self-explanatory photograph of an alternative way of transferring containers from road to rail and vice-versa. It was a simple and effective system, but the only disadvantage was that every container would have to be equipped with rollers to locate on the ramps.
Ian Allan Library

11
Miscellaneous Vehicles

All four railway companies operated a large number of odd types which come under the title 'miscellaneous vehicles'. Here, like the rest of the book, it has not been a case of what to put in but, due to space reasons, what to leave out. A small selection of some of the unusual types are shown here.

Above:
A classic photograph? This maintenance gang is about to undertake track repairs on a branch line, using rather primitive transport.
Quainton Railway Society

Right, top and bottom:
Among the fleet of road/rail tankers were small numbers of articulated tankers. To ensure stability while on rail flats, the trailers featured outriggers at the front and additional steel wheels at the rear, which matched up with supporting tracks on the rail wagon.
Ian Allan Library

Right:
The Karrier Ro-Rail bus was well known, but less publicised was a truck version of the idea used on the West Highland section of the LNER to carry permanent way workers and their supplies. When on the rails the road wheels were raised up and clipped into position, leaving the rail wheels on the inside making contact with the track. The operation was carried out at a level crossing. *Ian Allan Library*

Right:
Very little is known about this vehicle except it is a Bedford WH type fitted with Lewin section sweeper cleaning apparatus and numbered in the miscellaneous fleet of the LMSR. *Courtesy G. Arnold*

Right:
In BR days the parcels transported between the London terminal stations of the different regions had a fleet of Scarab and van trailers which could be distinguished by the black and white chequer pattern around the waist rail of the van body.
W. J. Aldridge Collection

Centre right:
The railway companies and indeed BR have operated cross-Channel ferries for many years. With the postwar growth of roll-on/roll-off ships and the movement of unaccompanied trailers there was a need for a number of shunting tractors. This is a 1967 example manufactured by Douglas.

Bottom:
The GWR used an American tractor made by McCormick-Deering Co of Illinois in the late 1920s. It is seen here hauling a Carrimore trailer.
Ian Allan Library

Facing page, top:
The railway companies used many different types of tractor for depot haulage and even shunting of railway wagons. This is an International tractor used by the LMSR in 1931 at Crown Street, Liverpool.
Ian Allan Library

A Rolls-Royce used by the publicity department of the LMSR. The car was registered in 1929, but may have been converted to a van at a later date, presumably before Rolls-Royce stopped such conversions being made.
Real Photographs

Right:
BR took delivery of a large number of these Bedford 1½-ton chassis with Spurmont 12-seat bodies for use by engineers and track maintenance gangs.
Ian Allan Library

Below:
Used during the 1950s and early 1960s, Rooks personnel carriers on the Commer 25cwt chassis were a familiar sight.
Ian Allan Library

Below right:
With half the body having 14 seats and half available for equipment, these BMC FG series vehicles were ideal for permanent way gangs, and saw much use at weekends and at night. *Ian Allan Library*

Above:
From 1957 BR took delivery of a number of these Karrier Gamecock chassis with special bodies for carrying 11 men and equipment used by engineers, mainly from the signalling department. *Ian Allan Library*

Below:
One of the latest types of vehicles used by engineers is this Bedwas-bodied personnel and cargo van based on a Leyland Roadrunner chassis. *Ian Allan Library*

Appendices

1 Liveries

It must be realised that these notes regarding liveries are a generalisation as there were many different variations, especially in the placing and size of letters. When it comes to colours it is sometimes difficult to define accurately a particular shade: black and white photographs are a great help, in showing the positioning of lettering, and will give a good idea of the size, but they will not show any colours accurately — certainly not any shades. Furthermore, one has to remember that the earlier photographs taken on ortochromatic film are different from the results with panchromatic emulsions used today, and they did show reds as near blacks, etc.

Most of the livery variations occurred during the wartime days, and many vehicles ended up in a plain grey livery; again, many had little or very simplified lettering.

British Rail

For the first two or three years the scene was a mixture with vehicles in the old leveries with the words British Railways painted on and the fleet number given a regional suffix (ie F 2828 E for Eastern Region, etc).

The first livery was an all-over maroon with the words British Railways spelt out in full in cream — this colour was also used for the fleet number, etc. The next livery lasted almost to the end and was the popular carmine and deep cream (better described as 'blood and custard'). The carmine was at the lower sides and the vehicles by that time had adopted the British Railways 'double sausage' logo, which was in carmine on the cream painted panels. There were a few cases where this

was applied in yellow on the carmine, but these were rare and did not last long. On flat trucks the wording 'British Railways' was in cream on the carmine sides.

The next livery change for the vans appeared in 1961 when some were painted an all-over 'stone' colour (a buff or fawn shade) with the words 'Rail Freight' in white and the peculiar arrow logo (known as the 'flying crate') in brown and white.

The final livery was an all-over yellow with the double arrow logo (often referred to as the 'arrows of indecision') in red.

Great Western Railway

At first the vehicles were painted an all-over brown and carried the words 'Great Western Railway' in 5in high letters painted white or cream. From about 1923 the familiar two-tone chocolate (plain chocolate colour) and cream appeared, with lettering in cream on brown, or brown on the cream panels. For a time the GWR 'button' roundel (in brown on cream) was applied to vehicles, as can be seen in some of the illustrations. Tipper trucks were invariably an all-over grey.

London Midland & Scottish Railway

From the early days of the horse-drawn vehicles the LMSR colours remained more or less constant. Crimson lake was used for the bodywork and black for the wings, tilt and any framing. The lettering was white on the black (or maroon), and occasionally gold or straw colour was used, and again there were cases where this was shaded red. Where lining was applied this was gilt or yellow. During wartime some vehicles were all over maroon, and even grey in the utility period.

London & North Eastern Railway

Prior to 1932 when the Gill Sans lettering was introduced, there was no official standard livery for LNER road vehicles, which tended to remain in the pre-Grouping colours. From 1932 however, the Royal Blue (ultramarine) colour was adopted and this was used for the main body of the vehicle, with black chassis and tilt. The lettering was in white. On some occasions the wheel centres were painted red and on some 1930s lorries the wording for the name was placed on a red panel. Postwar vehicles usually had the LNER oval totem in white.

Southern Railway

From the beginning, this was more or less a standardised livery, the body being a Maunsell dark green with yellow lettering and the wings, tilt and chassis black. There were some examples where the roof of the van and the cab were painted white; and there were a few examples of red wheel centres, but this is the excepton rather than the rule. In the late 1930s a slightly lighter shade of green was used and the lettering changed to white.

The livery for this LMSR parcels van was maroon on crimson lake below the waist-band with gold coloured 'LMS' and fleet number shaded bright red. Above the waist-line was black with white lettering, except the front (above the cab) which was gold coloured shaded bright red. *Ian Allan Library*

2 Fleet Numbering Systems

The various railway companies' vehicle fleet numbering systems make a fascinating study and varied from the numerical simplicity of the Southern Railway scheme to the complexity of the London & North Eastern Railway.

GWR

The Great Western initially used a straightforward numerical sequence — the higher the number the newer the vehicle. During the late 1930s this scheme was modified by using the first digit to equate with the carrying capacity of the vehicle, prefixed by a letter denoting roughly the type, but not make, of vehicle. The following example will indicate the pattern:

B 4401 four-ton Austin K4 Van
C 3621 three-ton Scammell Mechanical Horse
D 8890 eight-ton Bedford/Scammell tractor unit
E 2801 two-ton Douglas Electric Van

SR

Southern Railway lorries and vans were in a straightforward numerical series suffixed M for motor.

LMSR

The numbering system devised by the LNWR was continued and added to, and consisted of a basic numerical series of numbers suffixed by a letter to denote the type of service the vehicle was used on:

A
B Goods Vehicles
D Passenger parcel fleet
G Mechanical Horses
S Steam Waggons
X Others

Thus 440 D was a Fordson two-ton parcels van while 224 GD was a Karrier Cob mechanical horse used on the parcels service. 653 G was a Scammell Mechanical Horse for the goods service and 1754B was a Karrier GH5 also on the goods operation.

LNER

This railway had originally commenced with a simple numbered series, but as the fleet grew in strength and complexity a new system was introduced which instantly gave details of make, model, approximate gross capacity and fleet number. Therefore the following examples would apply:

MR 1105: Morris Van one-ton, fleet No 105
FA 7100: Fordson 7V, seven-ton, fleet No 100
FE 4180: Fordson B, four-ton, fleet No 180
EN 8100: Commer Superpoise, eight-ton, fleet No 100

A further modification was to use the first digit of the fleet number as an approximate guide to the location of the vehicle, thus:

EN 8000: Commer Superpoise — Scotland
EN 8100: Commer Superpoise — North Eastern Area
EN 8300: Commer Superpoise — Great Northern Area
HF 8112: Scammell six-ton Mechanical Horse, 8ton gross, NE Area, fleet No 12
HA 6301: Scammell three-ton Mechanical Horse 6ton gross, GN Area, fleet No 01

BR

When British Railways came into being in 1948 the immediate alteration was to enter a region code as a final suffix: W — Western Region, S — Southern, M — London Midland, E— Eastern, Sc — Scottish. However, confusing matters, in Scotland all vehicles were allocated in either the LM or ER fleets. Hence they retained their original LMSR or LNER number suffixed by Sc.

For a short while the Western Region added a number prefix to denote carrying capacity while the Eastern Region added a series of numbers to denote actual area of operation, such as:

6 TN 8302 E — London Area based, Thornycroft Nippy Artic
7 HK 6378 E — Norwich Area based Scammell Scarab three tonner.

A later modification was to alter the first digit in the four digit series to show actual carrying capacity so that the Scarab mentioned above became 7 HK 3378E.

In the mid 1960s a brand new numbering scheme was introduced for the whole railway fleet, based essentially on the LNER/BR (E) systems.

5 FB 5253 HS — five-ton Ford D Series based on the SR.
4 VA 2157 HM-Bedford J4/Hawson Walk-Thru Van based on the LMR.

The first suffix letter echoed the vehicle registration suffix, so that the first example above was YRK 253H and the second LJH 157H.

Unfortunately it has not yet been found possible to obtain a fleet list of all railway vehicles; portions of fleet lists do exist, but none of them give an overall picture. As a result we have to guess the numbers of vehicles that were purchased, how long they operated and where they were based.

Registration numbers

The registration letters used by the railway companies fell into several quite straightforward series. The Great-Western and Southern Railways after 1923 obtained their registrations in London. All LMSR vehicles were registered in Hertfordshire, often using a complete set of numbers such as BNK 1 to BNK 999. The LNER used London registration letters for those vehicles in the old Great Northern area while in the North Eastern area, York supplied the registration letters. Most Scottish vehicles had Glasgow registration marks.

A Scammell Scarab mechanical horse in BR livery which was previously operated by the GWR. The C prefix to the fleet number was the GWR code for a mechanical horse — the suffix W denoted Western Region.